Angry, Bitter, Broken, Unforgiving Until Jesus!

Who's that looking back at me in the mirror?

Joyce S. Owens

TRILOGY

A WHOLLY OWNED SUBSIDIARY OF **TBN**

PROFESSIONAL PUBLISHING MEETS POWERFUL PROMOTION

Trilogy Christian Publishers

A Wholly Owned Subsidiary of Trinity Broadcasting Network

2442 Michelle Drive

Tustin, CA 92780

10 9 8 7 6 5 4 3 2 1

Library of Congress Cataloging-in-Publication Data is available.

ISBN 979-9-89333-011-3

ISBN (ebook) 979-9-89333-012-0

Table of Contents

Introduction

"Who's the lady in my mirror?", this was the question that I repeated to myself after each surgery when I saw the new face appearing in my mirror. As you flip through the pages of this book you will see an angry, bitter, broken, and unforgiving lady whose fairytale had been turned into a nightmare. I remember my younger days, dreaming of my Prince Charming who would sweep me off my feet, carry me to my beautiful castle, and we would live happily ever after. But...Hey, isn't that what the movies and books teach us when we are growing up, but what happens when life's storms come and our dreams are shattered? How do we respond when our world is turned upside down? Do we stand firm on our principles and trust God, or do we become bitter? Life would be so much easier if we could just face all of life's storms while holding God's unchanging hand. As I look back over my life, my deepest regret was turning my back on God and allowing my storms to destroy me for so many years. Yet, it seemed like I faced storm after storm, wondering how or when it would all end. My life looked like a tornado had swept through and shattered every piece of me, leaving me broken. Instead of picking up my pieces and rebuilding, I began to give up. I was trapped in the prison that I had created, until Jesus picked me up and put all my broken pieces back together again. Jesus put a desire in my heart to draw closer to Him and to spend time in His Word. I began to shut myself in my prayer closet, closing off the world so that I was able to hear His voice. It isn't easy to humble yourself, admit your wrong, and turn it all over to God whom you hadn't trusted for years. But when you are down and have nowhere to turn, the only way is to look up. My advice to you is to take hold of His hand and trust that He can change your broken life. It doesn't mean your life will always be without storms; it just means you won't have to face them alone.

Dedication

First and foremost, I dedicate this book to my Lord and Savior. He never gave up on me. To Him, who knew my beginning and my end, who walked each step with me. He kept urging me to write this book, even when I wanted to walk away. Jesus, thank You so very much for loving me, for guiding me, and leading me when I wanted to give up. And yes, Lord, You were right, as always. Healing does come when we truly face ourselves, thank the Lord!

I also, want to dedicate this book to my beautiful daughters who went through the storms with me, facing a new mom, time after time. My love and appreciation cannot be expressed. Thank you both for being real troopers and staying with me, never giving up on me. You both have grown up to be beautiful mothers on the outside and the inside. Connie, with those beautiful curls, as a young child you looked just like Shirley Temple. That is a name your daddy called you by, and he loved you so much. He would be proud of the young lady you have become, going to college after your three children were grown and making the Dean's list. Your mom is so proud of you, and again thank you for being an incredible you! I love you so much, my Connie Leeco. Marie, my beautiful younger daughter who has grown into a wonderful young lady, who has four beautiful children and two grandchildren. Now you have decided to be a nurse. I know you are working so hard to complete school; yes, it's harder as you get older, but you have the determination. Do not settle for just doing it but to keep all A's, like your sister. I love you my dear child. Both of you girls make this mom proud to call you my daughters. You both weathered the storm and came out shining. Remember to do your best and do it all for the glory of God.

The Book

As I write this book, it is not something my flesh wants to do; but the God that dwells inside me has given me no rest. He kept bringing it to my heart to finish what I started many years ago. I had rather put it away again than relive my past, but healing comes when we face who we really are. When I was going through all the face changes and many surgeries, I searched for books to help me, but I was unable to find any resources to help. I said years ago if I could help only one person through my story, all the pain and heartache would be worth it. I believe God can use everything we go through to help others, if we only allow Him to. We live in a hurting world; someone needs to know that God is willing to help and heal. I was angry with God for many years, thinking He could change my face back and take all the pain away. Now, I see that through this journey I have taken, there was a purpose. God can use our brokenness to heal others. Somewhere among these pages, you may relate to something you are going through, something that is stealing your joy. Satan doesn't want us to heal; he has control as long as we live with our bitterness. My hope for each reader who is hurting, bitter, or broken is to allow God to heal them. God doesn't want us to live a life of brokenness. He can and will take that and make you whole again. At the beginning of this book, you will see that I didn't know who I was. I asked myself so many times, who was that looking at me in the mirror? My bitterness grew with each surgery, and after having over twenty different faces due to all the surgeries

God brought me face-to-face with my problem. It wasn't my outside but my inside that needed healing. I now know the lady in the mirror; a child of God, loved, healed, and forgiven. Now let's take this journey together, turn the page, and come face-to-face with who we are.

Every day, we get up and look in the mirror, or at least sometime during the day, we see ourselves in the mirror. Until decades ago, I had never given much thought as to how I identified myself by what I saw in the mirror. Our faces are what we look at and say, "This is me." When we see someone we know, it is their face by which we recognize them. On March 12, 1980, I looked at who I called Joyce for the last time. Early one morning, I was taken down to surgery; I looked at myself for the last time.

My story began in the summer of 1979 at a visit to a new dentist. As I was there to have my teeth x-rayed, he found a tooth that had never come through. Upon reading my x-rays, the dentist said it was in his professional opinion that I should see an oral surgeon. His office made my appointment that day. Also, I mentioned to him that I had a problem with biting my lower lip and that I had worn a retainer for six months, but it hadn't helped. He suggested that maybe I should see an orthodontist. At my first appointment with the orthodontist, he told me that he could help me, but I would need to wear braces for two years to correct the overbite. He also gave me the option to wear braces for three months, but if I chose to go that route, I would need surgery that only an oral surgeon could perform. The orthodontist explained that the surgery would consist of uncovering the tooth under the gum, and then he could lower the tooth and build a partial in between the missing tooth. He said that he and the oral surgeon would work closely together and both of them could compare notes and set a date for surgery within a month. I explained to him that I would like to talk this over with my husband before making a decision. During the month that followed, my husband and I made arrangements to meet with the oral surgeon to discuss the details of the procedure. The surgeon explained that he would take the upper maxillary and remove a tiny piece of bone, allowing him to move my teeth up and back. The procedure he suggested would correct my overbite and give me the results I desired. While in the surgeon's office, he shared with us the before and after pictures of the procedure. After speaking with the surgeon, my husband and I decided to move forward with the procedure, as he assured us it would be a simple procedure. Little did we know this would be the beginning of a nightmare.

As I look back on my childhood, it's hard to think that life would ever turn out the way it has. I was one of seven children; we lived in a small town where everyone knew one another. As a child, times were rough; we didn't have running water or indoor bathrooms. My father owned a small sawmill and was a preacher of a small-town church. Mother didn't work until the last of us seven children went to school. It was then that Mother went to work in a sewing factory. We wore hand-me-down clothes, and occasionally we would get a new dress. All of us had to pitch in and help to make ends meet. I remember my sister and I would carry slabs for fifty cents a day and work in the field when crop planting time rolled around. We lived close to my father's parents, so we were able to visit them every day; I was very close to my grandfather. I can still see his smiling face as we sat on the porch and listened to his stories. He was my hero!, I heard the phone ringing one quiet morning while still in bed. Then I heard my mother exclaim, "Your father has just shot himself." I jumped straight out of bed; my heart was in my throat. At first, I didn't think my father was home; I thought mother was talking about my father. When I reached the front door, I could see my daddy running down the road.

I discovered that it was actually my grandfather who had shot himself; he was dead! I loved my grandfather. I needed my grandfather. I couldn't imagine my life without him, but life did go on. I finished high school, got a job, and started my journey in the big world of working-class people.

Within a year, I met a handsome young man who played in a band. In the beginning, my parents didn't like him because of his lifestyle. We were brought up in a Christian home where you didn't go to the movies, dances, wear pants or shorts, or marry someone who had been married before. This young man was all of the above, and we were married five months later. We moved in with his parents in a neighboring town, life seemed complete. Now, I was able to do all the things my parents would not allow. We bought a small trailer, and a few months later and moved it onto his father's land. Every day I would go home and visit my parents. Mother had taken ill, and she wasn't doing well, this doctor had given her a few months to live. Her kidneys had deteriorated, and her doctors expressed that they felt that she was too old for a transplant. Every day I went up to stay with her, I feared she would be dead when I got there. Then one day, Daddy took her to see a new doctor at the state hospital. This new doctor said Mother wasn't too old and he wanted to do a transplant. My mother's sisters were all checked as possible donors, but the doctors decided to go with my oldest brother. The surgery was performed, but within a few days her body rejected the kidney transplant. The kidney had to be removed. Mother was then put on dialysis and Daddy learned to operate all the equipment so that Mother could be treated at home. He had to give up work to stay home and help keep her alive! He would have to put her on the machine three times a week. Every day one of us would fix her lunch and dinner. This went on for two years; meanwhile, I had a baby, and she looked just like her father.

Our marriage began to fall apart; little things became big things and we separated for a short time. While we were separated, my husband found out he had a brain tumor, and I chose to move back home to care for him. The tumor could not be removed, so the doctors didn't give him long to live. We had to travel every day from Toccoa, GA to a hospital in South Carolina to have treatments. I would work the evening shift at my job, go home to sleep a few hours, get up to drive him to the hospital, and get home in time to do it all over again. A little over a year later, my husband passed away. I am thankful that our little girl grew up to look like her father. He was a special man who will always be remembered.

My mother was not improving, and the doctors agreed that it was time to try another transplant. I had now remarried and lived in a much bigger town about thirty minutes south of my mother and daddy. The doctors decided to run tests on all of us children to determine if they could find a match for Mother's kidney. The doctors told us they preferred to use me as the donor because I was very slim, and removing my kidney would be less invasive. When the doctors ran the needed tests to check if I was a match, they discovered I was pregnant, and this ruled me out completely; my oldest sister was then chosen. All the tests were completed, and the surgery was performed. The surgery was a success! Mother's body did not reject the kidney this time. A few weeks after my mother's surgery, I had a miscarriage. I can't help but feel that God worked all this out so that Mother received the perfect match for her kidney, and only God knew it wasn't to be mine that needed to be used. It was hard to accept losing my baby, but the doctors said I could try again in a few months. I was afraid to try, I didn't know if I could take losing another baby. A year later, I had a baby girl who was born healthy.

Now here I was, married with two beautiful girls, living

in a nice home near the lake, and half-owner of a business in Atlanta! Honestly, I felt that my life had taken a turn for the better. Things were starting to look up, but not for long. I was going to have a surgery that would take everything I knew as my nice life and turn it into a nightmare with terrible consequences. The nightmare began on March 12, 1980, the surgery was to take only a couple of hours but ended up taking five hours. I wasn't supposed to need blood, but the bleeding was so bad that I would have to undergo a blood transfusion. The following day I remember waking up in so much pain and the surgeon who had performed my surgery telling me I would need to have my jaw wired together. He had mentioned before that this could be a possibility, but it probably wouldn't be needed. He asked my husband to take me to his office later that afternoon so he could wire me together there. It was pouring rain and very cold that day as my husband loaded me into the car and drove me to the surgeon's office. Later that afternoon, I asked to see myself in the mirror. Little did I know that I would be looking at someone I didn't recognize, unable to accept the stranger in the mirror staring back at me. I was told there would be some swelling, but my face was the size of a basketball. Of course, I did have hopes that it would look better once the swelling went down. Finally, the day had come that I was able to return home; boy, did this sound good! I missed my two little girls very much. At the time, one of my daughters was eight years old and the other was only two. I hadn't been away from them for this long and couldn't wait to get home. I hadn't thought about what my little girls would think when they saw their mother, who didn't look like the same mommy they had seen a few days prior. My husband and I pulled into the driveway, and all I could think about was seeing my little girls. Unable to talk because my mouth was wired shut, I wrote on a piece of paper and asked where my girls were. I didn't know that they ran and hid when they saw me walking up the stairs to the house because they were afraid of what they had seen. I looked like someone who had stepped out of a scary movie.

After my husband sat down the girls and explained to them the circumstances, they came to me, hugging me, and told me that they loved me. The problem was that I could see the fear in their eyes, and I began to cry. Later in my room, I began to see why the girls were so scared. Here was a woman brought home whom they were told was their mother, but she didn't look like their mom at all. My eight-year-old would hide behind the couch when I came around and state that she was scared. After a few days, the girls started to come around me on their own and love me without being told to do so. I was wired together so I would have to use a notepad to communicate with others around me; the problem was that my children couldn't read my writing. As the days continued to go by, I was able to get up and take care of the kids and the house. The oral surgeon had given me instructions to keep a warm compress on my face to help with the swelling. Weeks passed, and most of the swelling had gone down, and I looked like a very wrinkled old lady. I would sit most of the day looking in the mirror and crying. I was also losing weight because my mouth was wired shut, so I was unable to eat solid foods. The pain was still there, and breathing was almost impossible. My septum had been pushed over to the right side of my nose during the surgery, causing my air supply to shut off. The swelling had also cut off breathing much from my left nostril and trying to breathe out of my mouth was impossible. Each time I returned to see the oral surgeon, he would put a metal rod up my nose to try to move my septum over. Each time I would visit him, he would cause so much pain trying to move my septum over that I began to take pain medication before each visit. As time passed, the situation did not improve; if anything, it only worsened. I would not leave the house with the exception of doctor's visits. I hated for people to visit because I couldn't stand to see the look on their faces as it was like a shock of a shining light bulb staring at me. The pain of facing people was something I couldn't take, so I began to withdraw from everyone, including my family. I became so unhappy and depressed that I no longer wanted to live. One day, I overheard my husband talking to his brother on the phone, telling him I didn't even look human anymore and that he couldn't stand to look at me. Many times, I would wear a piece of cloth over my face so all you could see was my eyes. I had one comfort; my eyes were the only part of my face that looked like the person I used to know.

I was beginning to give up on life; I didn't want to live anymore. One day at the doctor's office, I mentioned to him that my life wasn't worth living anymore. He suggested that I talk to a psychiatrist, and promptly made an appointment for me. I went to see the psychiatrist, but this didn't seem to help. I had given up hope; life was like a broken piece of glass that couldn't be put back together. It was then that my husband finally started looking for another doctor who could help me. He found a doctor in Atlanta near our place of business and made me an appointment. This was five weeks after my first surgery; little did I know that many surgeries would follow. The doctor I was scheduled to see was a plastic surgeon. I spoke with the oral surgeon to tell him about my upcoming appointment with the plastic surgeon, and he expressed to me that he could do another surgery to fix things and make it all better. There was no way I would ever let this man touch me again! The oral surgeon would not admit any wrongdoing and insisted he continue performing the same surgery he had performed on me on others with the same problem. He then told me that I looked better now than I did before the surgery and that I should destroy all the pictures I had of myself before the surgery because no one would believe it was me. This made me furious! All I could think of was him ruining someone else's face the way he had ruined mine. Part of his statement to me was so very true; no one would believe that my pictures prior to the surgery were me, not because I looked so much better, but because now I looked like a wrinkled old ugly lady! When the oral surgeon realized I would not allow him to do another surgery on me, he suggested another doctor in Atlanta other than the doctor my husband had found, but there was no way I would even see a doctor he recommended! I now realized he was trying to send me to a doctor with whom he was friends, so that we would not know the truth about what he did wrong in the surgery he performed on me.

The day had come to go see the new plastic surgeon my husband had made me an appointment with. Early that day, before going to Atlanta, the oral surgeon had removed the wires from my mouth; it was a day I will never forget. My nightmare had come to life, I couldn't see my upper teeth at all. They were so far up that when I talked, it sounded like I didn't have any teeth at all. I looked like an old woman who had no teeth! I was only thirty years old. I used to see a beautiful young girl in the mirror, and now I was looking at someone I didn't know and didn't want to know. I cried all the way to Atlanta to meet with the plastic surgeon. All I could think of was, "Why did this happen to me?" How could anyone take and destroy someone in this way and yet say they did nothing wrong? I was so angry and bitter, not to mention the extreme pain I felt when I looked in the mirror. Who was this older lady? What was she doing in my mirror? Where was the person I wanted to see? I didn't know this person; I wanted the old lady in the mirror to disappear and bring back the beautiful girl who used to stare back at me. How could one's life change so much in only a few weeks?

The nightmare was real, and all I wanted was to wake up from it and find the person I was searching for in the mirror. I know it's hard to imagine how I felt; you must live the nightmare to understand where I am coming from. All my life, I had been taught to be content with life and to never question God about anything that was happening, but this was different. It's hard to be content when you no longer know who you are.

My tears and anguish were becoming a large part of my everyday life. I seemed to be crying more each day that passed. I thought to myself, can this new doctor help, or am I doomed to be this old lady at the age of thirty? I prayed that somehow, somewhere, there was an answer. We finally arrived at the plastic surgeon's office, and my eyes were now red and swollen from crying. My husband and I had brought pictures, molds, and files from the oral surgeon's office. As I met with the new doctor, he looked at the pictures, molds, and medical files. He then explained that he could try and correct the problem. He then had another group of doctors come in to look at me. Each of them agreed that another surgery should be performed for correction. A follow-up appointment was made to take x-rays and new molds of my teeth to prepare me for the surgery that would follow in a few weeks. The surgery would consist of taking a bone graft from my hip and bringing my teeth down. The surgery was scheduled for the latter part of May 1980. After this surgery things still weren't much better. My nose was still the same as it had been, I still had a hard time breathing and my face was flat! I was once again wired together so I was unable to tell if my teeth were brought down. I was released a few days after the surgery and was able to return home. By this time, I had learned to talk much better with my mouth wired together and discovered foods that I could put in a blender and drink that weren't half bad. Upon this discovery I didn't drop as much weight as I had during the first surgery, due to this newfound discovery. Before the first surgery, I weighed one hundred and ten pounds and now I was seventy pounds. Within a few weeks, things started to improve and I was able to go visit my mother, It was still too early to tell if the surgery had been a success. Seven weeks later and I went back to the hospital to have the wires removed, and it was then I discovered my teeth were still not far enough down. I was shocked! The plastic surgeon explained that during the surgery, he had discovered that the floor of my nose had been removed, and the septum had been cut off. I couldn't care less about what he was telling me. All I knew was that I wanted a change, and I wanted it soon. The plastic surgeon then explained that he would be able to repair what the oral surgeon had done, but I would have to be patient; it would take time. Patience had not been my strong point, so I had to learn how to be patient. After all these weeks of suffering, I needed help fast. The plastic surgeon said I would have to wait at least six months before he could perform another surgery. I didn't know if I could wait six months, but I would try.

I continued to see him during the six months for regular check-ups, and the day finally came to set a date for the following surgery to repair my nose. On September 3, 1980, I checked in to Emory Hospital in Atlanta, GA, to have the surgery. This surgery would consist of taking a piece of bone from beneath my right breast to rebuild my nose. When I was brought into recovery I was unable to breathe. If you have ever had surgery on your nose, you can relate. Your nose is packed with gauze, and you must breathe out of your mouth. The pain was almost unbearable, And the incision under my right breast hurt so badly that I could barely move. The plastic surgeon explained to me that with a bone graft, extra bone is needed due to shrinkage, so my nose would appear much larger for a while, but he could always trim it down. I now had another new face to cope with. I thought, Patience, where are you when I need you? Talk about ugly! I had a cast on my nose, just like a cast on a broken leg. Looking back, I can find humor in it, but at that moment, I found nothing amusing about it.

The surgeries kept coming, and in September 1980, I had a chin implant to balance my face. I was sinking further and further into depression. Each time I looked in the mirror, that ugly stranger looked back at me. There seemed to be no light at the end of this black hole. Then, the plastic surgeon suggested I see a dentist that did reconstructive work and would be able to fix my teeth. In October, I went to see the dentist, and after examining me, he suggested I first see an orthodontist who would work to pull my teeth forward. I then went to the orthodontist, who wanted to use a chin cup to see if he could get my teeth to move. I told him I would have to ask my plastic surgeon to make sure I could apply pressure to the chin implant I had just received. I was told by my plastic surgery that it would be fine. On November 5, 1980, my plastic surgeon performed another surgery to trim my nose down, and this surgery made me feel a little better. At least my nose wasn't so big and now had a much better shape. Thereafter, I went forward with the treatment plan the orthodontist had suggested, and a chin cup was applied. I know you are probably wondering, what is a chin cup? It's hard to describe; let's see, it looked like a horse bridle that you wear on the top of your head. There is a cup that fits on your chin with wires coming out from the cup that hook to braces that are applied to your teeth. I was to wear this crazy-looking thing all day and night except when I ate. I tried to get used to wearing that contraption, but it would give me horrible headaches. Within two days of wearing the chin cup, my chin was red, swollen, and hurting. I reached out to my plastic surgeon, who advised me to remove it until this cleared up. After a week, my chin was clear, so I put it back on. Shortly after, my chin started to get infected, and my plastic surgeon advised me to take it off and leave it off! December 15, 1980, rolled around; this was my birthday, and I wanted this nightmare to end. I was tired of all the surgeries. Who wouldn't be after seven of them? I thought, was there ever going to be an end? Now more questions... Who am I? What did I look like before? What has happened to me? Will I ever be happy again with how I look? So many questions and no answers. I had been through so much since March, and all I wanted was for this all to end. I remember looking in the mirror fifty times a day and crying, wishing I could turn back time and change everything back to the way it was before. On Wednesday, January 14, 1981, I went I followed up with my plastic surgeon on where we would go from here. He suggested I see a psychiatrist in the hospital at Emory to try and accept all the changes I had gone through. I began to see the psychiatrist on a regular basis. This would also help me cope with the many surgeries that were to follow. The next surgery would be performed by both my plastic surgeon and an oral surgeon who was a teacher at a dental school. The surgery was set on March 12, 1981. I didn't realize when the appointment was set that this was the same exact date my nightmare began, a year earlier. Thankfully, the oral surgeon couldn't make it on that date, so the appointment was changed to March twenty-fourth. Then March 12th rolled around; it was difficult for me. That whole day all I could think of was how I could go back a year and change things.

It was the following day, March 13, 1981, that I found out my husband was having an affair! He told me he was leaving me and he was planning to take our children away from me because I was so unstable. I should have seen this coming, but I was so wrapped up in my troubles that I was blinded to it. When he told me his plans, I begged him to stay. I promised him I would change and try harder. He said he couldn't stand to look at me anymore; I didn't look human, I was ugly, and it turned his stomach every time he looked at me. The following day, he left, and my my older daughter was visiting her grandparents. I called my best friend to see if she could watch my younger daughter, and after they left, I took a hand full of pills, and climbed into the bed. I was trying to end it all! My neighbor came over later that day to check on me and found me. All I remember is the next day waking up in the I.C.U. Upon waking, the psychiatrist I had been seeing came by to talk with me, but I was too angry! All I could say was, "Why wouldn't they just let me die?" My life seemed to have ended a year ago. I asked him if I could go home. His reply was "No way!" but I signed the papers and released myself anyway.

After arriving home, I started to do a lot of thinking. My life was such a mess and I wanted to close my eyes and have it all be over, but I realized that taking my life wasn't the answer. I was scared; in less than two weeks, I would be going through another surgery. This would consist of three different cuts and being wired together once again. What would I do with the girls? Who would be there to help me take care of them? My husband came to me and offered to stay until I could get back on my feet, then he would leave again. I didn't want him there after all he had said. He told me when I tried to kill myself that the one right thing I had tried to do was end my life and I was unsuccessful at that. The following Monday, my plastic surgeon wanted to see me as soon as possible. Upon arriving, my psychiatrist was there, they took me into an office and my plastic surgeon suggested that we cancel my surgery until a later date. After returning home from my appointment, my husband agreed that we should take a trip away from home to talk about things. We left on a

Wednesday morning to fly to the beach. I tried talking with him, but it was no use. He began drinking, got drunk, and told me he was in love with another woman and wanted out of this marriage.

We returned home the following day, and he moved out. For once in a long time, I felt relief. Now that he was gone, I wouldn't have to listen to how ugly and stupid I was. I wouldn't have to worry anymore about where he was or what he was doing. On Friday of that same week, I went to visit my psychiatrist. He agreed I should move forward with the next surgery because he thought it would help me. On March 22, 1981, Mother came to watch the kids. My best friend drove me to the hospital for my surgery. That night I was in my hospital room when I opened my suitcase and inside were two little notes from my mother, with Bible verses written on the page. She would never know how much these notes helped me that night.

Surgery was scheduled for early the following morning. My family and friends had finally stopped coming to visit when I was having surgery. But this time I could have really used someone. Mother was unable to be there because she was all I had to watch over the girls. I began to turn to the only One who had truly stayed with me through everything, and that was the Lord. He had always loved me through it all and was trying to help me if I would only let Him. After surgery, I was taken to the I.C.U., and all I remember is being in so much pain. The nurses tried to keep the tubes coming out of my side and my nose clear of fluid. The following day my doctors came by and removed the wrapping around my head, and requested I stay another night in the I.C.U. Once again, my mouth was wired together and I had stitches in my left hip from where the bone graft was taken to repair my nose. My whole body was in such terrible pain.

The next day I was taken to my room and the tubes were removed from my nose, which made me feel somewhat better, but the pain was still bad. I was trying to keep my mind clear and not think of the mess my life had become. So much had taken place in such a short period of time. What would I do now that my husband had left me? I would be wired together for another seven weeks, I couldn't work, I couldn't take care of myself, let alone take care of my children! How were we going to survive? I prayed and cried most of that day in my hospital room. Later that day, my mother brought the girls to see me. They had really been through a lot, and I didn't want my girls to see me like this; I still had tubes coming out of my left side and my face was still very swollen. Once again, this would be another face for my girls to accept as their mother. When they came in to see me you could see the scared look on their faces as they entered the room. My younger daughter wouldn't even come near me. I really didn't blame her, though; I wouldn't expect any child to want to come close to anyone who looked like I did, even if someone told them it was their mother. She kept repeating, "That's not my mommy." Here again was a woman they were told was their mother, yet she kept changing every time she went to the hospital. My older daughter was beginning to withdraw from me. She had lost her father when she was four, then had happily loved her new father, and now he had left her. She felt like everyone she loved, including her mother she used to know, was leaving her. I could see the hurt in her little eyes! My younger daughter didn't understand what was going on, but instinctively knew everything was not as it should be. I remember when I returned home from the hospital, my younger daughter would go sit on the steps and wait for her daddy to come home. I would go out and get her, and she would cry and say, "I want my daddy" and "when is he coming home." My heart was breaking for my children. I didn't know how to help them. I was still in so much pain from my surgery and my head was killing me. My life seemed to be a disaster!

After a few weeks, my husband finally moved all his belongings out. My children started to come around me, sit beside me, rub my arms, and say, "We love you, Mommy." I thank God for my children; they helped me hold it all together when I felt like my life was shattering into a million pieces. For ten weeks, my husband refused to send money, knowing that I was unable to work. His parents, who lived in another state, would call every week. When they found out my husband wasn't sending me money, they began to help me out with money to get food for my children. I went to see an attorney to file for a divorce and the attorney drew up papers for temporary child support so we could eat and have a little bit of money to pay the bills until the divorce was final. Two weeks after my surgery, my neighbor moved in with us to help take care of me and my children. When I was able, I took over doing all the cooking, cleaning, and taking care of the children. By this time, I was able to talk a little more clearly and the swelling in my face was going down. Even with my mouth wired together the girls were able to understand what I was saying to them. After all, I had been wired together for a total of five months in the past year; I was becoming an expert at mumbling clearly. Talking wasn't the only thing I had perfected, and I was pretty good at eating through a straw too. The one thing that really bothered me was all the food television commercials, you know the ones that show all that good food and say, "They are cooking one just for you!"

The follow-up with my plastic surgeon went well, but I was told I would need more surgery. I was so frightened I began to cry. Was this ever going to end? Would I ever have any peace? Was I condemned to more pain and agony for the rest of my life? I had never in my thirty years hated anyone until now, but I viciously hated the oral surgeon who had caused my world to collapse. I also felt much hatred for my husband who had walked out on me and my children when we really needed him; I had become very bitter!

Time passed and with God's help I began to live one day at a time, just waiting for the day I would go in for another surgery, or the day I would wake up and this would all be over. I prayed that it would be soon. I didn't know if I could go through another month, let alone another year. My emotions were up and down most days; I would have a wonderful pity party for myself and invite only me and all the different faces I had been. I once again fell back into my shell. My upper lip had shrunk so much that I looked like a grimacing monkey. The only place I would go was to visit my mother. I wouldn't let anyone see me. People would call and I would make excuses to not have them around. I mentioned this to my plastic surgeon, and he told me after I had healed, he would do another surgery to lower my upper lip. I didn't want to wait, but I knew that I would have to. All these surgeries I have mentioned were just in the first year and a half. I would have no idea that within the next eight years, I would have over twenty-five more! To list them all would make a book in itself.

After all my surgeries, I am now married to a wonderful man who loves and accepts me just the way I am. My ex-husband married on the day of our divorce and is now divorced again and planning to remarry again soon. When my older daughter was nineteen, she had been married and had a child of her own. My younger daughter, at age twelve, had a few problems, which I blame on my past and all that she has had to go through. I pray to God that our years ahead will be brighter and that one day I will be able to love and accept the person who is looking back at me in the mirror.

As you read the first chapter of my journey, you can see how bitter, angry, broken, and unforgiving I was. It was all about losing my looks and not knowing the lady in the mirror. It was not knowing who I was anymore every time I had surgery. There was a different lady in the mirror for many years of my life, a face I didn't like and didn't want to get to know. At that time all I could see was the outside, and believe me, it was all messed up. My many faces were also affecting my inside. I was drifting, depressed, and broken; my life was shattering into a thousand pieces. I kept wondering when this would all end. I had so many faces to face back then and my children had many moms to face.

All of this had affected me and my children over the years. For many years I had tried to write all of this out but would quickly put it down. I didn't want to revisit this part of my life and I was ashamed for others to see this side of me. I was also ashamed that it took me so many years to realize that it's not about the outside, it's the inside that God wants to change. God didn't see the ugly lady; He saw His child whom He loved. Many times, we are so consumed with how we look and how others see us. I, too, was consumed by my appearance. I was so angry at my husband for walking out on us when we needed him most. Yet, looking back, the one I really needed had never walked out on me! He promised in His Word He would never leave or forsake me.

Deuteronomy 31:8 - *And the Lord, He is the one who goes before you. He will be with you, He will not leave you nor forsake you; Do not fear nor be dismayed.*

Yet I had forsaken Him! I let the past and present destroy my life and the lives of those around me. It's funny how we allow the world to show us how we should look, and how we should dress. Don't get me wrong; I believe we should look our best, but not be consumed with how others see us or like us. If only we were consumed with the way God sees us! He thinks we are beautiful, yet I must admit, my outside was all I could see, and I didn't like what I was seeing. Consumed by my looks, wanting to go back and relive the time before my first surgery, thinking if I could just go back to the eleventh of March and back out of the surgery how different my life would be. But even though we would all like a do-over at some point in our lives, we cannot go back. Once a day is behind us, we must move forward. We can't change our past, but we can make a change for our future by making better choices, not worrying about pleasing man, but pleasing God.

For years I was so wrapped up in my looks on the outside that I let the inside go. I was feeding my outward, fleshly man and starving my spiritual life. See, God doesn't expect us to look like a beauty queen. He wants us to focus on Him, and let our lives shine, living a life that our inside grows more and more and we allow God to increase inside of us. Always remember we are beautiful in God's sight. I know there are many who are unhappy with their looks, maybe with scars on the outside or a defect that bothers them. I am not downplaying the pain you are feeling. I realize that each time you look in the mirror and you don't see what you might think is beauty, it bothers and hurts you. You just want to change your looks. Often we seek plastic surgeons, try make-up, or even products that promise to improve us. If who I am explaining is you, my heart goes out to you. I spent many years wearing a mask, even before COVID. All you could see were my eyes. My eyes were the only thing about my face that I knew. I felt so ugly and hated myself. For all the new products on the market with the promise to erase our wrinkles and spots, there is not a product for helping us with our self-esteem. God loves us too much to leave us like we are. That is why He went to Calvary so we could live a happy life, a forgiven life, an eternal life.

Building walls of protection: As I faced more surgeries, I began building walls; I wouldn't let anyone but my family and closest friends in. God didn't intend for us to be alone. He is for families and fellowship with others. I've withdrawn so many times in my life out of security and pride, thinking I was unlovable, which was Satan's lie. My wall needed to come down. I felt it was my way of protecting myself from being hurt again. It is not easy to build a wall; it takes time. Mine was one brick at a time, and I had no plans to remove my wall. It was my hiding place, my protection. Understand, building walls isn't done overnight, especially when you have disappointment and hurt from one storm after another and you can't see an ending to all your brokenness. My wall was very high; I had to shut the world out. All the pain after every surgery caused me to spend most of my days alone and crying. The pain medication would take away the physical pain, but it couldn't heal the pain I felt each time I would look in the mirror at a different face.

After all the surgeries were over, I began to allow God to tear down my wall. The day had finally come to put my past behind me and return to my family and my church. These were the people in my life who didn't treat me badly or think I was ugly. I was the only one who felt these feelings about myself. I began to get involved with the church again, teaching Sunday School, teaching kindergarten in the Christian school, singing in the choir, directing Bible school, writing articles for the local church paper, visiting nursing homes, creating bulletins for the church, and many other things. I really thought these things would get me God's approval after I had been so angry, bitter, and unforgiving for so many years, but you see, God loved me and all my works were in vain. As long as I kept my anger, bitterness, and unforgiveness inside God couldn't use me in the way He wanted to. In everyone's eyes, I was a hard-working member of the church, yet I was still so broken. I had been raised in the church since birth so I could play the part. I knew how to teach the Word of God and point the children to Him. I heard a preacher once say, God will allow us to help others, but we won't minister to Him in our sinful condition, and this was true in my life. I believe there are a lot of people, like I was, living the same way today. We attend church and hold positions in the church, yet we are holding on to things in our lives. I was still so broken, bitter, and unforgiving, thinking I could operate and live a life pleasing to God's will. Everyone looked at me as a good Christian, but they couldn't see the real me inside. They had seen my outward appearance, but I was still wearing a mask. When asked how I was doing my reply was always, "I'm doing fine." Deep down inside, I wasn't fine; there was still anger, brokenness, bitterness, and unforgiveness. It was easier to escape all these feelings by covering them up. If you had met me back then, you wouldn't have seen the mess I was in.

It's amazing how many people wear masks every day; never showing how hurt or broken they really are. Broken homes, broken relationships, broken children, all messed up on the inside. Everyone at one time or another has had things on the inside that no earthly person could see. We smile, we blend in, we are almost perfect, yet on the inside hidden away are our sinful actions, sinful thoughts, the other side of us. We think no one sees, but God sees and He wants us to repent, turn our lives over to Him and make a new life in Him. Yet I couldn't. I held on to all my anger! How could I turn all these things over to God? Anger and bitterness had become a big part of who I was. I looked at other Christians' lives, and I wondered why it seemed they all had so much peace. I'm sure their lives had ups and downs too, they had just learned how to leave it in God's hands. I wanted that peace, yet I couldn't, or should I say, wouldn't forgive. I prayed and I wanted to forgive but then I would see my ex-husband who had walked out on me when he would come to get our daughter for weekends, and the anger would come right back. I can now truly say I have forgiven him. He is now married for the seventh time, so I realize it wasn't all about my face. I can now pray for him and hear his name and not feel anger. You know when you truly forgive someone their name or face doesn't anger you anymore. You want the person to get saved and wish them good, not bad. Years ago, while writing this, I couldn't say that, it's only now that God has healed that part of my life. I would love to say that everything is great all the time, but I am human, living in a fleshly body, and still make bad choices I have to repent of daily. God is so faithful and good! He has taken this broken piece of clay and put it back together on the Potter's wheel. And to think the life I thought was so shattered and not worth living for, He turned around. I had to revisit all the past I had held on to so tightly, and then to understand that by holding on, these things steal your joy, peace, happiness, hopes, and dreams.

Wasted Years: Being brought so low, I could only look up has taught me that I have wasted so many precious years. There is no way to go back and change the past, and I now wonder if I could have made a difference in someone else's life that may have been battling a similar situation. If only we could learn early in life to leave things in God's hands and allow us to heal. Satan sometimes reminds me of my past, but I remind him that Jesus has forgiven me and set me free from my past. If you have things you need to lay at Jesus' feet, give them up. You will never find true happiness and peace until you allow Jesus to heal you!

Writing my story of how I survived and overcame all that has taken place in my life is one of the hardest valleys

I have had to battle. Over the years I gave up everything; it seemed to be easier than reliving all the pain. As a preacher's daughter, it should have been easy to lay all my hurt, anger, and unforgiveness at Jesus' feet. Yet I felt I could keep all of this and still serve Him. I've walked through many years crying and begging God to please let this cup pass. God has a purpose that only He can see. For over forty years, He's been waiting for me to surrender. Now I see I needed to write this for my healing, and I am convinced that someone out there who needs healing is waiting on this story. I am not a writer; English and literature were not my best subjects. I have fasted and prayed over this book, wanting it only to bring glory to God, to help others see that God is more than able to take all the broken pieces of our lives, put us back together, and make us whole again. *A Broken Vessel in the Potter's Hand* was the first title I planned for this book, but God had another plan, so the title was given by Him. May you find the healing you need to be able to accept who you are and love the lady (or person) in the mirror.

We Can't be Part-time Christians:

Matthew 6:24 - *No man can serve two masters: for either he will hate the one and love the other: or he will hold to the one and despise the other.*

As this verse says, you cannot serve God and Satan at the same time. God doesn't want us part-time, or just half of us, He wants all of us. He didn't partly pay for our sins or say He would pay for half of our sins. He said He paid for all our sins, and we owe Him all of us. That would be like saying, "I will marry part of you, but not all of you; I will love you when you're perfect." Jesus died for all our sins and loves us unconditionally. I am so thankful for unconditional love, because if God didn't love me unconditionally, He would have given up on me a long time ago. I know if it had been me, I would have walked away and had nothing to do with me, but Jesus never left me even when I walked away from my precious Savior.

2 Peter 3:9 - *The Lord is not slack concerning his promise; as some men count slackness; but is long-suffering to us-ward, not willing that any should perish, but all should come to repentance.*

Unconditional love is hard; we don't mind loving the people who love us, or the people easy to love.

In Matthew 5:43-44 we read, *Ye have heard that it hath been said, thou shalt love thy neighbor, and hate thine enemy. But I say unto you love your enemies, bless those who curse you, do good to them who hate you, and pray for those who spitefully use you and prosecute you.*

This is a hard verse to swallow. We don't want to love those who have done us wrong or treat us badly, yet Jesus says to love your enemy. I have made so many wrong decisions, yet my God was patient with me. He patiently waited, knowing my beginning and end. All the times I held on to my anger and unforgiveness, God could have given up on me. He could have said to me, that's it, you've reached your sin limits, you're on your own now, but he knew that one day I would be able to tell this story and help others see that he is faithful and patient with us. Never wanting anyone to perish, Jesus came to heal the sick and broken, which I was. I must admit I still have a hard time with my outward appearance, but with God's help, I am healing. I used to joke and say, "Well, I don't have to wear a paper bag over my head anymore." But the lady in the mirror has been a real struggle. I just have to remember He's still working on me. We will all have many mountains and valleys; some will have much sorrow and heartache. God never promised our journey would be easy, just that He would never leave or forsake us.

I used to think being a Christian would be an easy life, but Jesus told us in His Word, John 16:33, *These things I have spoken to you, that in me you may have peace. In the world you will have tribulation; but be of good cheer, I have overcome the world.* John 15:18 says, *If the world hates you, you know that it hated me before it hated you.*

Once we are saved by God's grace, we are changed. We do not belong here in this world; it's not our home. We are new creatures in Christ. (Therefore, if any man is in Christ, he is a new creation. The old things pass away, behold, all things become new. 2 Corinthians 5:17.) When we accept Jesus as our Lord and Savior, it doesn't mean we are to sit around and wait for Jesus to take us home. We should be telling others about Jesus, working to help build His kingdom! We are to be His hands, His feet, His mouth to a lost and dying world. As I look back to my younger years, I realize God had a purpose for my life. It wasn't for me to be angry, bitter, and unforgiving, but to use me for His honor and glory. I failed Him so many times and walked my own way, yet He was faithful. He saw and knew who I could be if I would only surrender and allow Him to work through me. My deepest regret is my wasted years, but we can't live in the past. We must move forward to be better, make a difference, and allow Jesus to use us.

Broken Vessel: God can't use an unwilling vessel. If you have a vessel that is broken, it can't be used; it is the same with our lives. We are unusable if we remain in our sinful condition. For many years I was an unusable vessel. My bitterness and anger were affecting my health. In 2010, I had to have triple bypass surgery, which was probably a result of all the stress in my life. My older daughter had run away from home, and my younger daughter, at thirteen, was using drugs. Things once again seemed to be falling apart. Six years after my bypass surgery, I found out my husband had stage four lung cancer that had metastasized to his brain. I was so stressed out. Yet God was there with me to help me through it all. Are you an unusable vessel, broken and unwilling to be put on the potter's wheel? It is not easy to become a usable vessel; it takes being crushed, molded, and going into the fire. Many valleys, mountains, and heartache; but think of all the souls you could point to Jesus if you were a usable vessel.

Caregiver: Before my husband's diagnosis, we moved his father to our in-law suite and took care of him for ten years. Praise God, at the age of eighty-seven he accepted Jesus as his Lord and Savior! God has blessed me with the gift of being a caregiver. I also took care of a lady with dementia for three years. I was aware of death; I had moved, at one point, to Florida to take care of my mother-in-law after she lost both of her legs, and I watched her die. I watched my father-in-law die, my own father, my mother, and two of my spouses. Losing close loved ones is hard, but it doesn't mean we throw in the towel and just give up. I think about Joseph in the Bible, he was thrown into a pit by his brothers, sold into slavery, and accused of something he didn't do, then cast into prison. God was faithful; Joseph was taken out of prison and made second to the king. Nothing stops God's plan! Joseph had every reason to throw in the towel and give up, yet he stayed faithful, believing God would keep His promise. Also, Job in the Bible, lost everything, his children, his wealth, and his health. Yet he too remained faithful to God. I know many people, including myself, who have gone through many valleys and come out in victory, though it took me so many years. I fought God, I didn't want to trust Him, even though in my heart He was trustworthy. And to think, all this was over the change in my looks.

I am so ashamed that I allowed Satan to keep me in my prison for so long. Today, Satan has no hold on me! I have given all my brokenness, anger, unforgiveness, and bitterness to Jesus. I am so grateful that my loving, long-suffering God had mercy and patience with me. He drew me unto Him and healed my brokenness. I know if it weren't for the grace of my almighty God, I wouldn't be here today writing this book; I would still be on the path of destruction. It wasn't until I gave everything to Him that I was able to find peace, joy, and happiness. True repentance means to change, walk a different way, not to stay on the old path, but to be renewed. I know have a purpose in my life, something I thought I would never have. My face may have changed to the point I didn't know who I was then, but I know now: I am a child of the King who loved me, forgave me, and restored me. Praise God! If you are in a storm and you feel like life has no purpose or feel like ending it all, please don't lose hope. Jesus is standing with His arms stretched out to receive you and give you a new purpose., a new journey that will give you peace in the midst of the storm. Read God's Word, find a Bible-believing church, and let God help you draw closer to Him. The family of God will love and accept you, pray with you, and walk with you in your newfound faith. Remember, there has never been a searching, willing vessel that God can't change and give saving grace.

Now here is a subject many don't want to discuss. For many years of my life, no one knew about the sexual abuse I had endured as a young child. I kept silent, afraid to tell anyone, afraid no one would believe me. I was only a child, and I really didn't understand what was happening to me; I was being sexually abused! They would tell me not to mention to anyone what they were doing to me. It wasn't until my adult life that I ever spoke a word of it to anyone. This strongly affected my life; I thought all men were out to hurt me. My way of dealing with what had happened to me was hurting others. I would accept a date with men and turn around and stand them up. I would accept a man's proposal to marry, then call it off. It's a wonder that I ever even got married. My trust level in men was a big fat zero! When I finally married, I was subjected to mental and physical abuse; I would leave but always go back. I was insecure and believed it was always my fault. There was a time in one of my marriages I left with two black eyes, and I swore I wouldn't go back. It's crazy how I always seemed to return to the abuse. I watched my younger daughter later on in life go through abuse by her second husband. He fractured her jaw, threw her around, bit her, and kicked her out. I would go get her only to watch her go back. Abusers only cause insecurity. They will break you down so they can have complete control if you allow them to. As the abused, you always think to yourself that you can change that person, but God is the only one who can make a change in someone's heart. Then there is the mental abuse, which I believe is worse than the physical abuse. A physical wound will heal, but words get into your mind and the hurt can remain in you. You may be able to forgive, but to forget is much harder. Forgiveness is like a wound; it will heal, but you still have a scar. If you find yourself in an abusive relationship, I urge you to tell someone and seek help. God doesn't want us to remain in an abusive situation. There are many resources out there that are easy to find with all the technology we have today. I'm not saying it will be easy; believe me, it's not. Now, I know healing takes time! I spent so many years not being able to trust men. It followed me way into my adult life, but God has helped me, and He can help you too. I still have scars, but I can say now I have forgiven my abusers. Abuse is a part of your life that will remain in your memories, but it cannot control you if you give it to Jesus. Forgiveness is not saying what was done to you was not wrong, but forgiveness is what will set you free. Sexual abuse or molestation is never the fault of a child, even though as a child, I didn't understand. I felt dirty and was afraid of my abusers. I now know it wasn't my fault. At the time I could only feel ashamed, but the healing process begins when you trust in the Lord and give your hurt to him.

Jesus said in Luke 4:18, *The spirit of the Lord is upon me because he hath anointed me to preach the gospel to the poor, he hath sent me to heal the brokenhearted, to preach deliverance to the captives, and to set at liberty them that are bruised.* When you are abused, you are bruised. Forgiveness to one's abuser will take time, but it is possible. In Jesus, there is healing and freedom. Call out to God; He can heal and restore. Nothing is impossible with God. Luke 1:37 states, *For with God, nothing is impossible.*

We live in a fallen world, which started in the Garden of Eden when sin entered the world. We are all children of Adam until we accept Jesus into our hearts. The Bible tells of how the journey of God's children has been hard; we are not promised a smooth and perfect life while we travel through this world. I look at how far we as a nation have drifted away from God. It has to hurt our God to see the world He created for the good turn against Him when He loved and knew us before we were ever born. Jeremiah 1:5 NIV reads, *Before I formed you in your mother's womb I knew you, before you were born I set you apart and appointed you as a prophet to nations.* My prayer is that our eyes and hearts are open to help change the world. We need to learn that change comes when we allow our love, kindness, compassion, and prayers to draw us closer to Him.

Anger, Bitterness, Forgiveness:

The Bible tells us in Ephesians 4:26, *Be ye ANGRY, AND SIN NOT; let not the sun go down on your wrath.* Wrath is

34

great anger that expresses itself in a desire to punish someone.

The Bible's definition of wrath is synonymous with anger, as told to us in Proverbs 15:1 NIV- *A gentle answer turns away wrath, but a harsh word stirs up anger.*

Wrath is known to be one of the deadliest sins. What makes it so deadly, you might ask? Transgression! Wrath can be summarized as strong, vengeful hatred or resentment, which causes us to act irrationally. Being angry over things going on in our lives is a human reaction, but allowing anger to get out of control, to cause our sin, is when we find ourselves wanting revenge, to get even with someone who has hurt or betrayed us. As human beings, we have all had times in our lives we have gotten angry, but when we allow the anger to get out of control, we become bitter. We think of ways to get back at that individual for hurting us.

We see a lot of anger in today's society, such as in school shootings. These are usually caused by angry people; someone has hurt them, and getting even means punishing everyone, even the innocent. We have given a place for evil thoughts to creep in. In society today, people are selfish, only thinking of their own gratification in vengeance, but vengeance is mine, sayeth the Lord! (See Romans 12:19.) I blame a lot of the evil in the world today on video games, movies, and the internet. We allow our kids access to all the evilness, to see such violence and murder that they have become numb to it. No compassion! Young minds aren't developed enough to separate fiction from non-fiction. The evilness is even being slipped into our children's cartoons today and is going unnoticed by adults. This is done with the purpose of destroying our children and unleashing evil inside them.

To remove the bitterness and anger from a person is to allow God to reveal it within you and remove it from your life. God can take all your anger from you and replace it with good things if only you allow Him to. It is okay to be angry over sin and wickedness in this world, but not to the point that we seek revenge or try to correct it in an unlawful way. Instead, we must pray for the wicked.

I can honestly say that throughout my journey in life, I had allowed my anger to turn into bitterness and hate. All I thought about for many years was getting even with those who had hurt and betrayed me.

I John 4:20 states, *If a man saith, I love God and hateth his brother, he is a liar; for he who loveth not his brother whom he hath seen, how can he love God whom he has not seen?*

I wanted all who had betrayed me to suffer as I had. I knew these feelings were sinful and wrong, but bitterness had taken control of my life. The thoughts of getting even were not hurting the ones who had hurt me, but rather killing me! The bitterness and hatred werehurting my health, my family, and most of all, my relationship with God. See, bitterness and anger go hand and hand, and if left unchanged, they will eventually destroy your life and the lives of those you love. Anger is mentioned 455 times in the Old Testament. 375 of these are used to explain God's anger. When God sees evil, He experiences anger. Anger is a logical response to injustice.

In Ephesians 4:31-32we read, *Let all bitterness, wrath, anger, clamor, and evil speaking be put away from you, with all malice. And be kind to one another, tenderhearted, forgiving one another, even as God in Christ forgave you.*

My years of anger, bitterness, and unforgiveness took

many years of my life that I cannot get back, but although I cannot change my past, I can change the future. Be a light to others who are struggling with anger and bitterness and point them in the path of Jesus. I remember an illustration told to me years ago that stuck in my mind; it was about a man who had a big garbage bag that was full and heavy. He carried it everywhere he went. He would sit down for a while, but then get up and grab his heavy bag and continue to carry it. People asked him, "Why do you keep carrying that heavy bag? Why not just get rid of it?"

He would reply, "It's mine and I just carry it." In the illustration, it was his sins, hurt, pain, anger, and brokenness he was carrying. He refused to put it down, so he carried all this burden for years until one day Jesus said to him, "Let me have that bag. I can carry all the garbage you have in there and get rid of it if you only surrender it to me." See, we carry all our guilt, pain, anger, and burdens around when Jesus says we don't have to.

Matthew 11:28-30 NKJV says, *Come unto me all who labor and are heavy laden and I will give you rest. Take my yoke upon you and learn from me; for I am gentle and lowly, and you will find rest for your souls. For my yoke is easy and my burden is light.*

Jesus can take all the garbage you are carrying and give you new life. Why not give all that garbage to Him? He is big enough to take it and clean you up.

I was in a prison of my own making, carrying around all my garbage, but Jesus took the key, unlocked the prison door, and set me free. I am not proud of my past, but I have been forgiven by the blood of Jesus! I had made so many mistakes and wasted so many years, until Jesus broke down the walls I had built and set me free. I wrote a song after I was delivered that said…

> I am so glad, Lord, that You never gave up
> on me. You waited and waited patiently. With
> Your arms wide open You said, "Let me come
> inside." I am so glad, Lord, You never gave
> up on me. So, I let You come inside, Oh, what
> peace Your love provides; where my heart
> was black with sin, now Your love abides
> within. You came and washed me white as
> snow, now my heart overflows. I'm so glad,
> Lord, You never gave up on me.

> Since I've been set free, I'm living the latter
> years of my life praising and worshiping my
> Lord and Savior. This song helped me to
> realize God can take anyone in their darkest
> moment and turn it around for their good!

It has been a long journey thus far, and as I read my Bible, I realize that God has given us a map, a guide, to follow. Years ago, I didn't study the Bible as much as I do now. Many people say the Old Testament isn't for us today. I beg to differ; it tells us of our future. It shows us how God was so faithful, how He is longsuffering and only wants the best for us, to trust and worship Him, to follow and obey His Word. We have all sinned and come short of the glory of God. In

Romans 3:23 we read, *For all have sinned and come short of the glory of God.* God is love; do not allow the world to convince you differently.

No one loves you more than God, who sent us His only begotten Son to die for our sins, as we read in John 3:16. *For God so loved the world that he gave his only begotten son, that whosoever believeth in him should not perish, but have everlasting life.*

John 10:10 states, *The thief cometh not, but for to steal and to kill and destroy; I have come that they might have life and that they might have it more abundantly.*

If we, as children of God, could grasp hold of His words and realize that just because we are going through storms and valleys in our lives, God still loves us and He is not punishing us, He's preparing us. Let Him guide you forward; let's not dwell in the wilderness. There is someone out there waiting to hear your story of redemption, your story of deliverance, your story of God's everlasting grace that saved your soul! Now as I close out this book, let me say there were many years I had happiness during my storms, before all the pain. I want to share a few with you. The birth of my beautiful daughters, and all my grandchildren and great-grandchildren. They have given me many years of love, joy, and laughter. And there were times in my younger years, one that pops up in my mind is growing up on a farm, we children always had to help out. One day Mom sent me to gather eggs. I didn't want to go, but I knew better than to say no. We had this mean, I mean, mean rooster. So, as I gathered the eggs I kept my eye on him, and he kept his eye on me. As I turned to leave, he began to chase me. Leaving the chicken cage, I began to run with that old, mean rooster right on my heels. I slipped and fell and when I did, he flew right on top of me and began to spur me. My screaming and crying brought my mom out running to my rescue. To make a long story short, we had chicken and dumplings that night for supper. There were other fun days in my younger years as well.

Daddy believed in having family devotion each night. We would all gather in the living room. Daddy would read the Bible, and we would all pray together. Growing up in a spirit-filled home, I should have reacted differently when my life began to fall apart. There was no excuse for the way I allowed Satan to use the storms in my life to cause me to be unusable. I have learned God can mend and He always forgives a repentant heart. God has been using my broken life to help others by bringing broken people into my life that I have been able to help through my testimony. God doesn't waste our pain; He uses it to mold us into what His desire for our lives should be. See, no matter what you have been through, there is always someone out there who needs to hear your testimony and know that you understand their pain. If I had never been through all the pain and heartache, how could I have helped others? So, I urge you to look at your life and all you have been through as a way to help someone else. There are a lot of people who are broken and in need of someone like you to help guide them. You can't always help everyone. There will be people who don't want to help themselves, but God knows the people to send that your story will help. Surrender all and remember, some people come into your life for a reason; some for a season, and some for a lifetime.

> I read this the other day and it was so real to me:
>
> Grapes must be crushed to make wine.
>
> Diamonds form under pressure.
>
> Olives are pressed to release oil.
>
> A seed must be broken to grow.
>
> God is turning your pain into something beautiful, trust the process, trust God! This is from a sermon by Billy Graham.

So, as I look at my past, I realize that God is turning my hurting, broken life into something beautiful.

I was in my prayer closet one morning praying, and Jesus said, "Do you trust Me?" I went silent. Did I really trust Him? I know for years I never trusted anyone, never wanting to be hurt again. The question cut to my heart. I searched my heart all day. Before the day was over, I could say, "Yes, Lord, I trust You." It's crazy how we often lose trust. Most people have been hurt by either a friend or a spouse. It is easy to lose trust. Everyone wants to be trusting, but when it comes to serving God, how trustworthy are we, and do we really trust God? I hear people say, "If God is so good, why did He let my loved one die," or "I don't trust God because He gave me cancer." We seem to blame God for anything we don't understand, or anything that is bad. I know I did back when going through my storms. I blamed God not just for my face, but also when my fifteen-year-old ran off with her boyfriend, and my thirteen-year-old started using drugs. Then when my husband ended up with cancer, I was so ready to give up. My first husband died from cancer when I was in my twenties, and now my husband of over thirty years had cancer. It's so hard to understand when someone you love begins to slowly lose their strength and die. The older we get, the more we experience our loved ones passing away. It doesn't ever get easy, and it is so hard to understand living in a fleshly body. It seems like when we don't understand, we blame God. Now I realize we are living in a fallen world, and storms will come, and life hurts, but I've learned that Jesus loves us, and sent us the Comforter, the Holy Spirit, to help us through these storms. I had the same mindset; why would God allow all these things in my life? God never promised bad things or storms wouldn't come into our lives, but He promised that He would be with us no matter what happens in our lives. This is a wonderful promise from God, and I have never seen God ever break a promise. (Proverbs 30:5, Every word of God is pure, he is a shield unto them who put their trust in him.) He is so trustworthy! No matter how dark our lives become, we can know Jesus still loves us and wants to shine us up. Yet we refuse to let Him work in our lives. We think we can make it on our own and only call upon Him when things get completely out of control. We only use Him when it is convenient for us. We live and walk the way we want until storms hit, sickness hits us or our family members, then we ask God to help. We are living in a time where we need God in our lives; there are so many hurting people, so many lost people. Are we going to stay asleep and let our loved ones perish? Today more than ever, we hear God's name being used in vain. It's in our TV shows, in our movies, and it's an everyday language for people today, using God's name as a curse word. How sad and how fallen we as a world have become when we use His name in vain. The third commandment says, "Thou shalt not take the name of the Lord our God in vain, for the Lord will not hold him guiltless who takes his name in vain." Yet, every day you hear his name being used as a curse word or a swear word. The closer I've come to my Lord, the more I have noticed it everywhere, movies, little children, grown-ups; in my day people respected the name of God, but not today!

The road map (written in 1997)

There is a roadway in the Bible. It tells of the state we are in. It tells of two roads you can travel. It tells where your journey will end. On the right you will find the road is narrow; not many want to travel this road. This road has many storms and valleys, and the road is rough to travel. On this road, Jesus will be with you, and at the end of this road, Heaven awaits you. On the broad road, many will travel. It has lots of room for everyone. Many choose this road because it's easy, but at the end of this road lies your doom. For you see, this road was made by Satan and he is waiting for you to reach the end. It is there the flames of Hell will be your destination. There are two roads; which one will you take?

God still speaks today.

I've heard God speak in my spirit so many times. You see, you want to be able to hear Him speak if you are not in His Word and talking to him daily. Let me tell you, a couple of times when He spoke there was no doubt it was Him. When God told me to finish this book, I told him that since I had moved to another house, and I had no clue where the thirty-one pages I had written years ago were. The last time I had seen them was before my husband died and they were in the basement of the house we lived in. The children had cleaned out the basement and I didn't know where the pages were or if I still had them. Then in my spirit, I heard a voice say, "Look under the stairs in the closet." It was there I had stored a few containers, and the first container I opened, on the very top, lay the folder with all my pages, including my before and after photos. And guess what the date was I found them? It was March 12, the same date the first surgery was performed. Many say that was a coincidence, but I know it was God!

In 1996, my younger daughter had been on drugs for so many years, and if you have had a child on drugs you will relate to this story. Whose child, God's child! The other night I was downstairs on my knees praying. I said, "Lord, You know my child has gone astray; she's living far away from You, and out in sin." I must have gone on for hours. "See, Lord things just keep happening over and over again; will there ever be an end?" Through tear-stained eyes, I heard my Savior say, "Whose child?" In my spirit, He said, "I only let you help Me when she was born. I put her in your care to teach and guide, but she belongs to Me. She's My child, so leave it all with Me." As you know, it's so hard to take our hands off. We want to solve everything on our own. This is where it comes in; we have to lay that child who's on drugs, living so far away from God, who's a prodigal child at the foot of the cross, and leave them in Jesus' hands. I know how hard that can be, but if you leave them in His hands, there will come a change. Don't give up on God, because He won't give up on you; just trust Him.

I work with a group of ladies in a mission called Angels in Waiting. We stop everything we are doing at ten o'clock in the morning, and pray for our prodigal children. We have already had two on our list saved. Praise God! I realized that night I was praying for my child years ago that God is in control. How many times do we pray for our children, and plead for them, cast them down at the feet of Jesus, only to pick them back up again when we realize we truly trust in Him? I know we are praying for our children daily, and we plead the blood of Jesus over them, but do we really believe He can take care of them? Just the other night, I got news that one of my grandchildren was involved in a very sinful thing. I stopped and prayed, praying when I walked outside, praying when I came in.

I felt so downcast. I picked up my Bible and when I opened it, it was on Jeremiah 32:17 (Lord God behold, thou hast made the heaven and the earth by thy great power and stretched out arm and there is nothing too hard for thee) and in verse 27 (Behold I am the Lord, the God of all flesh: is there anything too hard for me?)

A question I had to face was, is there anything too hard for God? I say nothing is too hard for my God, and there is nothing in your life that is too hard for God. He created the world in six days. He can handle anything the enemy tries to send our way. Why do we doubt and not trust that He can take care of anything we have going on in our lives? Some would say He can't take care of everything, but I would have to disagree. There is nothing my God can't do. He can perform miracles and wonders beyond your greatest imagination. Some say, "I have never seen a miracle," I would say to them to look in the mirror because you are one! Miracles happen every day; we just don't see them because we aren't looking. We have blinders on. Just look back at your life. I bet if you think about it, you can remember times when God changed something in your life. If you have a child, for instance, that in itself is a miracle of God. A child grows inside your body, comes out breathing, and grows up to become an adult. Your heart that's beating inside you each morning when you wake up and start your day is a miracle. You are a miracle created in the image of God. You see, God performs miracles every day; just look around you at all the beauty of the world, the flowers, waterfalls, etc. We live in a world surrounded by miracles.

Pray

Let us all come together and call upon His name, laying down our foolish pride and humbling ourselves at his feet. Only in His presence can we find comfort, rest, and peace. Joy beyond all measure can only be complete when we lay our sins and failures down at Jesus' feet, asking for forgiveness, mercy, guidance, and strength to make it through every day. Pray for protection and wisdom to discern and walk in God's perfect will. We can't make it one step on our own; we need the Lord to guide us and allow the Holy Spirit to show us the way. As we wake each morning and at the close of the day, come into His presence and give Him all the praise. We need to thank Him for salvation and know we would be nothing without our loving Lord. Don't rush out each morning to face the day alone; remember, things go better with God. So, put your ARMOR ON!

Ephesians 6:11-17 says, *Put on the whole armor of God, that ye may be able to stand against the wiles of the devil. For we wrestle not against flesh and blood, but against principalities, against powers, against rulers of the darkness of this world, against spiritual wickedness in high places. Wherefore take unto you the whole armor of God, that ye may be able to withstand in the evil day and having done all to stand. Stand, therefore having your loins girt about with truth, and having on the breastplate of righteousness, and your feet shod with the preparation of the gospel of peace. Above all, taking the shield of faith, wherewith ye shall be able to quench all the fiery darts of the wicked. And take the helmet of salvation, and the sword of the spirit which is the word of God.*

There were many days I never prayed or read my Bible. It was only every once in a while, when things became unbearable, that I did. With this kind of prayer life, you will never draw close to God. We need to stay consistent and pray daily if we truly want to walk closely with Him. 1 Thessalonians 5:17 says to pray without ceasing. That doesn't mean we spend all day on our knees crying out to God. It means to always have our minds on things of God, to have constant communication with Him, and always pray for God's will in your life. When you put on the full armor of God, you can fight all the evil things this world throws your way. As you live from day to day, your life is a book people read. What are you showing others? Will they read faith, hope, and love? Will they desire to have the same? Or will they see anger and bitterness? Let's allow our lives to show the world and those around us that there is hope, joy, and peace through Jesus Christ.

If your life was an open book for all the world to read, what would they read? I know you are reading a lot about my life, my mistakes, my anger, and my bitterness, but as you see my story didn't end in despair. It isn't a nightmare anymore, but a life brought back to life. A prison door opened, and a free child of God walked out with a new walk and mindset. My heart belongs to Jesus now; He is my light and guide. I will claim no other name but His name. Jesus is in my heart; He saved me! He paid the price long ago on Calvery's hill. It is there He bought my soul and my freedom. Even through the storms of life, He will be my guide. He said He would go with me and be my light. He left the Holy Spirit inside me to guide me every day. Storms will come, but let our lives make a difference in someone else's. See, God doesn't waste pain and suffering; He uses it. Sometimes we don't understand all we go through; life is full of lessons, and that's how we learn. I know during a storm it's hard to believe anything good could come out of it, but trust God. He will turn it into something beautiful.

After reading this story, if you are going through storms and you have never given your life to Jesus and are trying to make it on your own, give your burdens to Him. Jesus is waiting!

Romans 10:13, *For whosoever shall call upon the name of the Lord shall be saved.* Romans 3:23, *For all have sinned and fall short of the glory of God.* John 3:16, *For God so loved the world that he gave his only begotten son, that whosoever believeth in him should not perish but have everlasting life.*

Pray "Lord, I am a sinner in need of forgiveness. I ask now for Your forgiveness. Come into my heart, I believe You are the Son of God who died for my sins. By faith, I receive You into my heart. Save me and write my name in the Lamb's

Book of Life. Help me to live for You. In Jesus' name, I pray, Amen." If you have prayed this prayer, welcome to the family of God. Begin reading God's Word and pray.

Ministry I work in

Years ago, I was at church one Wednesday night when a young man walked by me carrying a bag that looked like it had cotton candy in it. I asked him if he had cotton candy in the bags, and he said, "No... they are baby blankets." As he showed them to me, I said to him, "Those are too small to be baby blankets." He explained to me the blankets were for stillborn babies or babies that had died shortly after birth. Then he told me of a ministry his mother had started at her house; it was called, Angels in Waiting 91:4, a non-profit ministry. They take donated wedding gowns and make dresses for babies who have passed away. I was blown away. I told him I could make blankets, so he gave me a card and asked if I would be interested in coming to see what the ministry was all about. I am so thankful I went. Boy, you would have to attend to really see what we do. It's a healing ministry. We take wedding gowns and men's ties and make beautiful gowns for mothers and fathers to put on their babies. It means a lot to the families; the baby they had hoped for and longed for is now gone. We are there to help them heal. You should read the letters we receive from the parents who receive our donations, thanking us. You see, it's not about us; it's about Jesus who led our director's heart to start this mission. It is truly a blessing! We pray over every wedding gown that comes in and every baby gown that goes out. We deliver them to the NICU units of hospitals and funeral homes all over the United States. We make the gowns as a labor of love. No one ever pays for these gowns; we are using the ministry to heal broken parents who have lost their little angels. I have researched how many babies are stillborn and have found that it affects 1 in 175 births, and every year

21,000 babies are stillborn in the United States http:/cdc.gov facts. That's 21,000 parents who are hurting over losing a baby, and that isn't counting the number of miscarriages. Research suggests that about thirty percent of pregnancies end in miscarriage; that's a lot of hurting parents need to know they have support.

Here are the words written by our director…

Angels In Waiting 91:4 exists to take donated wedding dresses and transform them into beautiful Angel Gowns for an infant's journey to meet our Lord and Savior. The ministry seeks to usher souls into the presence of the Holy Spirit through divine healing, deliverance, and spiritual growth through discipleship.

This ministry was born in 2016 after a lot of prompting by the Holy Spirit. It was once said by a very wise person that your purpose is birthed out of your greatest pain. I lost my first son in 1985 shortly after birth. Brandon only lived a short time, but he had such a huge impact on my life, and he was largely the inspiration for beginning this journey. I also lost a set of twin girls years later that were also a very big part of starting this ministry. The reason I started Angels in Waiting 91:4 is to help families just like me to cope with the loss of a child and to point them in the direction of Jesus Christ for their healing.

I remember the pain of having to make decisions for a funeral service instead of taking my son home to his freshly painted nursery. I remember having to settle for doll clothes to bury my son in because there was nothing made for him to wear for his burial. It was the collection of all the little pain points coupled with the excruciating pain of losing my baby boy that ultimately led me to start this ministry. I didn't have anyone to talk to, or anyone to help lead me on a path to healing. By providing an Angel Gown for a baby to go home to their Savior and by providing keepsakes in remembrance of that baby, I hope the families that are touched by this ministry can find their own path to healing from such a tremendous loss.

The book *Father Gives and Takes Away* was written about the ministry of Angels In Waiting 91:4, but it has a number of stories of the ministry has touched lives of those who have experienced the loss of a child. I wrote this book to help these families know they are not alone and that there is healing on the other side of brokenness.

To learn more about what we do and who we are, please visit www.angelsinwaiting914.com.

Closing

In closing, I would like to remind you that Jesus is the answer to anything you face. Matthew 11:28 (Come unto me, all ye that labor and are heavy laden, and I will give you rest. Take my yoke upon you and learn of me; for I am meek and lowly in heart, and ye shall find rest in your souls. For my yoke is easy and my burden is light.) Don't try to walk in this life alone, or carry all your burdens.

So many times I felt alone, so many times I felt defeated, so many times I had no hope, so many times I couldn't pray, so many times I walked away, so many times I felt forsaken, so many times I wanted to give up, so many times I felt lost, so many times I felt angry, so many times all seemed hopeless, so many times I felt broken, so many times I felt bitter, so many times I couldn't forgive others, so many times I felt invisible, so many times I felt life was over, so many times I played the part, so many times I wore a mask, so many times I was afraid, so many times I felt useless... Until Jesus showed me that I wasn't who I thought I was. He saw more in me than I could ever see in my own life. I will never regret turning all my sometimes over to Him so He could lead and guide me. No matter how far you have walked away from God, the return trip is only one step away. Remember, difficult roads lead to beautiful destinations. Isaiah 43:19 (Behold I will do a new thing. Now it shall spring forth, shall ye not know it? I will even make a road in the wilderness and rivers in the desert.) Proverbs 3:5-6 (Trust in the Lord with all your heart and lean not on your own understanding. In all your ways acknowledge him and he shall direct your path.) My prayer for you is to trust and leave it all in the Father's hands. As I have said before I am not a writer, I'm just a child of God who is thankful for Him loving me when I was unlovable. I have had a hard time getting my feelings and thoughts on paper. It was frightening, revisiting my past and all the emotions I felt throughout my journey in life, but if my story could help one person it was all worth it. My dad used to say I was going to be a missionary, and believe me, I ran from that calling, so I thought. Yet God brought me so many hurting, broken people who I could tell of His love and about salvation. So, as I see it, I've never been to a foreign country, but I became a missionary in my own circle of people. It's funny how we can try and run like Jonah in the Bible, but we can't run from God. He's seeing and knowing, the beginning and the end. His plan never fails, and when we give Him full control of things in our lives, everything begins to fall into place. So, here I am about to be 74 years old in a few days, and I fought about this book for 40 years. I pray that in some way it has helped someone to see that if your life seems broken and shattered, there is hope, it's Jesus!

In His hands,

Joyce

Psalms 37:23-24 (The steps of a good man are ordered by the Lord: and he delighteth in his way. Though he fall, he shall not be utterly cast down: for the Lord upholdeth him with his hand.

Our lives are like puzzles; each piece has to be placed correctly to see the full picture. Not all the pieces are the same. Some are small, some have corners, but all must be placed in the right place. We can't force a piece where it doesn't fit in an area of our life if it's not meant to be there; it has to be the right piece. Have you ever worked on a puzzle for days or weeks and then you realize that you can't complete the puzzle because a piece is missing? In our lives we can search, trying to complete our puzzle called life, and there is just something missing. That something is Jesus. We try to solve our own problems, we put on a happy smile, we search for something, yet we fail to feel complete because the most important piece is not there. God made us to be complete in Him. Without Him, our puzzled life would never be complete.

Printed in the USA
CPSIA information can be obtained
at www.ICGtesting.com
LVHW011540240824
789107LV00007B/202